Bearing Fruit

LIVING ROOTED IN CHRIST

A SOUL INSPIRED BIBLE STUDY

BEARING FRUIT SCRIPTURES

31-DAY SOUL DEEP SCRIPTURE READING LIST:

1. Psalm 1:3
2. Psalm 105:34
3. John 15:1-2
4. Isaiah 37:31
5. John 15:5
6. Matthew 13:23
7. John 12:24
8. Romans 7:4
9. Titus 3:14
10. Psalm 92:12, 14
11. Hebrews 13:15
12. John 15:8
13. Matthew 7:17
14. Romans 6:22
15. Matthew 3:8
16. James 3:8
17. Luke 8:14
18. Philippians 1:11
19. Colossians 1:10
20. Galatians 5:22-23
21. Ephesians 5:9
22. Philippians 4:17
23. Romans 1:13
24. Luke 6:43-44
25. Proverbs 11:30
26. Matthew 13:22
27. Luke 3:9
28. Romans 6:21
29. Ephesians 5:11
30. Mark 4:19
31. Proverbs 18:21

Additional Scriptures:
2 Corinthians 9:10-11

CONTENTS

BEARING FRUIT SCRIPTURES

31-DAY SOUL DEEP SCRIPTURE READING LIST:

1. Psalm 1:3
2. Psalm 105:34
3. John 15:1-2
4. Isaiah 37:31
5. John 15:5
6. Matthew 13:23
7. John 12:24
8. Romans 7:4
9. Titus 3:14
10. Psalm 92:12, 14
11. Hebrews 13:15
12. John 15:8
13. Matthew 7:17
14. Romans 6:22
15. Matthew 3:8
16. James 3:8
17. Luke 8:14
18. Philippians 1:11
19. Colossians 1:10
20. Galatians 5:22-23
21. Ephesians 5:9
22. Philippians 4:17
23. Romans 1:13

24. Luke 6:43-44
25. Proverbs 11:30
26. Matthew 13:22
27. Luke 3:9
28. Romans 6:21
29. Ephesians 5:11
30. Mark 4:19
31. Proverbs 18:21

Additional Scriptures:
2 Corinthians 9:10-11

VERSE MAPPING

First, know that there is NOT a wrong way to do this. The purpose of the exercise is to wring every little bit of meaning and application out of a scripture.

Second, while the writing portion of verse mapping is focused on a single, or small selection of scripture, know that the study process goes well beyond a single scripture reference.

1. **Read the verse.**

2. **Write out the verse.** (in the box, leave plenty of space around it, between the lines and between the words.)

3. **Personalize it:** replace words like "you", "we", "us", "them" with your name, where applicable

4. **Mark, circle, underline, highlight words** and phrases that stand out to you.
   - Any words make you want to dig deeper? Look up and define any words that need clarification.
   - Any promises from or actions of God?
   - Any action encouraged or required on your part?

6. **Read the verse in context**: read the preceding and following verses or whole chapter. See how it ties in to the verses before and after it.

7. **Read the verse in other translations**: note which words or phrases help you understand or apply the verse.

8. **Cross-reference the verse:** find, list and read other verses which speak about the same topic.

Bearing Fruit : Living Rooted in Christ

Read Galatians 5:22-23

- Place a mark next to the good fruits which others see in your life. Circle the fruits which need more nourishment.

____ love   ____ joy   ____ peace

____ patience   ____ kindness   ____ goodness

____ faithfulness   ____ gentleness   ____ self-control

- What is something specific you can do to increase the production or quality of these fruits in your life? Write it down, set a goal and hold yourself accountable.

Read Galatians 5:19-21
- Which, if any, of these bad fruits are present in your life?

- Is there something you need to prune from your life to eliminate this bad fruit? Own it, write it down, set a goal and hold yourself accountable.

THE HEALTH OF OUR SOUL
... "its leaf does not wither" ...

Wither and fall off. We see some trees go through this cycle of losing their leaves every autumn. But for evergreens, this withering and falling off only happens when the tree is unhealthy or dying from lack of nourishment.

A tree can lose its nourishment for a variety of reasons
* it becomes damaged or broken from the trauma of a storm,
* it becomes stressed by disease,
* it becomes overtaken by pest or outside invader.

This can happen in our own lives as well.

Life circumstances can damage us spiritually and as a result we might disengage from relationship with God.
* we overschedule our calendar and put aside reading our Bible
* we experience hardships and blame God
* we have a disagreement with someone and let bitterness infest like a devouring insect

* What things have interrupted the flow of nourishment from God into your own life?

_____ disappointment   _____ jealousy   _____ distractions

_____ bitterness   _____ hard times   _____ hurt feelings

_____ unforgiveness   _____ busyness   _____ pride

_____ anger   _____ _____   _____ _____

* Focus in on just one of the items you marked above. Which of your own actions have fed its development?

Bearing Fruit : Living Rooted in Christ

THE RESULT OF OUR FAITHFULNESS
... *"in all that he does, he prospers"* ...

To understand this last portion of today's scripture, we must first understand what the Bible is meaning by "prosper".

We make an enormous error if we infer the world's definition of prosperity – health and wealth – over the Biblical meaning in context of this scripture.

The word "prosper" here is not a label for money, finances, acknowledgement or fame. "Prosper" here refers to being prosperous or successful as it relates to fulfilling our individual purpose.

What is a tree's purpose? *To bear fruit*, whether literal fruit or by providing seed for other trees. If the tree stays rooted in its life source, it will prosper, it will be successful, it will achieve its purpose – *it will bear fruit*!

Likewise, if we stay rooted in our spiritual life giving source, if we remain faithful in relationship with God, the natural result will be the achievement of our kingdom purpose – *we will prosper*!

- What does kingdom success or fulfilling your purpose look like?

- In what way(s) have you seen God enable you to successfully fulfill your kingdom purpose?

Acknowledging what kingdom success looks like helps us to not get distracted by what it is not.

Bearing Fruit : Living Rooted in Christ

PRAYER

*He is like a tree planted by streams of water that yields
does, he prospers. Psalm 1:3*

its fruit in its season and its leaf does not wither. In all that he

DYING TO LIVE

"Truly, truly, I say to you, unless a grain of wheat falls into the earth and dies, it remains alone; but if it dies, it bears much fruit." John 12:24

I can almost see the confusion on the faces of Andrew and Philip. They went to tell Jesus there were visitors and he responds with talk of farming and lonely wheat and dying to bear fruit.

Huh?

We have a different perspective today than they did then and we know Jesus was talking about his own death, burial and resurrection.

The farming-wheat-dying-fruit analogy He gave also applies to his followers today.
1. Just as it was an image of Christ's literal death, burial and resurrection, it is also an image of Christian's literal death, burial and (eventual) resurrection.
2. It is also an image of Christian's spiritual death to self, being rooted in Christ and reborn to bear spiritual fruit.

PLANTING THE GRAIN
... *"unless a grain of wheat fall into the Earth"* ...

We are the grain of wheat mentioned in today's scripture. But let's consider the life span of an actual grain of wheat.

Seed —> planted in soil —> roots & first leaves form —> roots & leaves grow —> grain heads develop —> wheat is harvested —> seed gathered —> planted, etc..

To simplify even further, there is planting, dying, growing and producing.

It does seem odd to have dying in the middle of the life-cycle instead of the end, but somewhere in the middle, what was planted dies and becomes something else.

- Looking at the grain life span and considering it to represent your spiritual growth, where in the process are you?

- What do you need to do to grow into the next stage?

"Seeds are sown and rot but are far from perishing. Rather they grow up more beautiful. They are sown naked and dry and spring up green from death by the power of God." - Geneva Study Bible

DYING TO SELF
... "but if it dies, it bears much fruit" ...

Dying to self is part of being "born again" when the old self dies and the new self comes to life. (John 3:3-7).

In practical terms, it can be described as putting aside what we personally want in the moment to focus on loving God. It moves us away from self-centeredness and closer to Christ.

- So what does this look like in our lives?

⇒ We no longer try to get our own way (to gain attention)
⇒ We stop trying to impress others (to be elevated)
⇒ We stop offering unasked for advice (to feel important)
⇒ We no longer are obsessed with ourselves

"It is much easier to pay attention to the needs of others when our own interests no longer consume us." Jan Johnson

- What does dying to self look like in your life?

- Do you struggle with any of the descriptors above?

- How does this impact your ability to bear fruit?

> *"Part of the life we find and the fruit we bear is not only living a richer life with God, but also becoming more generous to others, reaching out to them with love and joy."*
>
> Jan Johnson, BillyGraham.org

Bearing Fruit : Living Rooted in Christ

CAN'T DO IT ALONE
... "unless a grain falls into the Earth it remains alone" ...

Right in the middle of today's scripture three words grabbed me - "unless" and "into" and "alone".

The processes of planting the seed and dying to self may explain where the action occurs, but they can't be done alone. There must be a catalyst, a stimulant, a food source.

In order to bear fruit, we must be "into" our food source, and our food source is God.

> *"Abide in me, and I in you. As the branch cannot bear fruit by itself, unless it abides in the vine, neither can you, unless you abide in me. I am the vine; you are the branches. Whoever abides in me and I in him, he it is that bears much fruit, for apart from me you can do nothing" John 15:4-5*

"fruit - *karpos* - everything done in true partnership with Christ, i.e. a believer (a branch) lives in union with Christ (the Vine). By definition, fruit results from two life-streams - the Lord living His life through ours - to yield what is eternal." - HELPS word study

- How connected are you to your spiritual life source?

- Make a recommitment to God, to put aside your personal desires and to focus on God and his will for your life.

NOTES

unless GRAIN -a- FALLS into the earth AND DIES · it REMAINS ALONE —but— IF IT DIES IT BEARS much Fruit John 12:24

VERSE MAPPING

PRAYER

Truly, truly, I say to you, unless a grain of
but if it dies, it

wheat falls into the earth and dies, it remains alone;
bears much fruit. John 12:24

NOTES

I AM the true vine & MY Father is the vine-dresser... and every branch that does bear fruit He prunes – that it may bear more fruit.

JOHN 15:1-2

FRUIT OF THE SPIRIT

"But the fruit of the Spirit is love, joy, peace, patience, kindness, goodness, faithfulness, gentleness, self-control; against such things there is no law. And those who belong to Christ Jesus have crucified the flesh with its passions and desires." Galatians 5:22-24

In our study we've examined a portrait of a healthy fruit bearing tree and learned how we must die to our self (sin nature) in order to be true fruit bearers, so now let's look at the spiritual fruit our lives can bear through the in-dwelling of the Holy Spirit.

Upon first read of today's scripture, we tend to consider each fruit as separate from the other and take the label "fruit" to actually mean "fruit**s**". But this is not the case. Paul refers to the fruit as a singular whole, like a bunch of grapes. All fruits coexist together as a single unit.

They are also a by-product of our relationship with God through the indwelling of the Holy Spirit. Meaning, as we cultivate this relationship, the fruit—as a whole—will naturally be produced.

The order of the nine fruit may seem randomly listed at first read, but they can actually be separated into three groups.

Love * Joy * Peace: The first three are *inward fruit and are relevant to our relationship with God.*

Patience * Kindness * Goodness: The next three are *outward fruit and are specific to our relationships with others.*

Faithfulness * Gentleness * Self-Control: The last three are more *general traits of a Christian, reflecting personal character.*

INWARD FRUIT-RELATIONSHIP WITH GOD

THE FRUIT OF LOVE

"This is my commandment, that you love one another
as I have loved you." John 15:12

agape love : unselfish love of one person for another.

Love is listed first because love is the foundation for all of the other fruit. And as with all of the fruit, Christ is our example for how we are to love others. (Romans 5:8)

What does the fruit of love look like in action? Is it fluttery butterflies and valentines and roses? Not exactly.

- Read 1 Corinthians 13:4-8a, then mark the attributes of love in your life:

_____ is kind	_____ does not envy
_____ is patient	_____ does not boast
_____ protects	_____ is not proud
_____ trusts	_____ does not dishonor
_____ hopes	_____ is not self-seeking
_____ perseveres	_____ not easily angered
_____ never fails	_____ keeps no record of wrongs
_____ rejoices in truth	_____ does not delight in evil

- Circle the attributes of love which have room to grow in your life.

- Select one attribute of love you circled - what seed can you sow to develop this fruit?

THE FRUIT OF JOY

"Rejoice in the Lord always, again I say rejoice." Philippians 4:4

joy : inner rejoicing in-spite of outward circumstances.

Joy is not like happiness which is conditional to what is happening around us or whether or not things are going the way we want. No, joy is present even in the midst of trials and suffering. Where happiness is an emotion, joy is an attitude of the heart that develops from love and the knowledge of God.

Because of this, even when our situation may appear hopeless, we can still choose to rejoice, knowing that our current situation is temporary and our salvation is eternal.

• What prevents you from experiencing this type of joy? What can help you to 'choose joy'?

The Bible also tells us that joy comes from being in God's presence.

"I have set the Lord always before me; because he is at my right hand, I shall not be shaken. Therefore my heart is glad, and my whole being rejoices; my flesh also dwells secure." Psalm 16:8-9

• How can you spend more time in God's presence?

THE FRUIT OF PEACE

"Peacemakers who sow in peace reap the fruit of righteousness."
James 3:18

peace : inward harmony with and trust of God's authority.

Jesus laid down his life to bring peace and reconciliation between sinners and God; and when we take that message to others, we are peacemakers.

This is different from our traditional understanding of peace keeping or the absence of conflict with others. Often our efforts are directed more toward keeping the peace by remaining silent instead of making peace through speaking God's truth. We have mistaken unity through silence as peace.

However, the separation Christ performs of the redeemed from the sinners causes division. Just as a shepherd separates his sheep from the flock.

Jesus tells us, *"Do not think that I have come to bring peace to the earth. I have not come to bring peace, but a sword." Matthew 10:34*

• How can having the fruit of inward peace help you experience outward peace in the midst of less than peaceful circumstances?

OUTWARD FRUIT-RELATIONSHIP WITH OTHERS

THE FRUIT OF PATIENCE

"Good sense makes one slow to anger, and it is his glory to overlook an offense." Proverbs 19:11

patience : a calm temper which bears evils without discontent.

Patience, here as it relates to others, calls for great wisdom and discretion. In being slow to anger, we take the time to truly consider the offense instead of reacting immediately and without restraint.

This cooling off allows the Holy Spirit to help us see objectively and react in a manner more Christ-like .

- Which of these tips might help when you are becoming angry?

_____ go for a walk   _____ listen to relaxing music

_____ do deep breathing exercises   _____ count backwards

_____ visualize a peaceful scene   _____ turn on positive thoughts

_____ meditate / read scripture   _____ _____

Our ultimate goal is to forgive.

"And Jesus said, "Father, forgive them, for they know not what they do."..." Luke 23:34

In other words…. *Let it go….. Let it go …*

- Is there someone in your circle you need to forgive for an offense? Ask God to help you forgive the offense.

THE FRUIT OF KINDNESS

"Be kind & compassionate to one another, forgiving one another just as Christ forgave you." Ephesians 4:32

kindness : act of goodwill which promotes the happiness or welfare of others.

Salvation produces true courteousness, not a hollow politeness. Our kindness should be the result of love and genuine good-will toward others. This is also the source of our compassion.

• Have you had someone be particularly kind to you? What did they do?

We are reminded again that the forgiveness of an offending brother is not something that we can neglect. We must remember that God has forgiven each of us more than we can forgive each other.

"See that no one repays anyone evil for evil, but always seek to do good to one another and to everyone." 1 Thessalonians 5:15

• Have you been in a situation to want to get even with someone?

• What is something kind you can do for them instead?

THE FRUIT OF GOODNESS

"So then, as we have opportunity, let us do good to everyone, especially to those who are of the household of faith." Galatians 6:10

goodness : reaching out to do good to others, whether or not it is deserved.

It should be our business to harm no one, and to do what we can to minister to the needs of others with any assistance that we can provide.

We're told to provide this support to everyone, whether our neighbor or stranger, whether rich or poor, whether Christian or not. But reminded to give special attention to not neglect our fellow Christians.

Each of these **outward fruit of relationship with others**, *patience, kindness and goodness*, require us to place the needs, and consideration of other before ourselves.

We must lay down our hurt feelings, our desires, and even our resources. Doing so of our own will can seem impossible. Thankfully, we do not have to depend on our own will, but rather the strength of God.

"I can do all things through Christ who gives me strength." Philippians 4:13

- Is God speaking to you about one of these fruit? What is He saying?

CHARACTER FRUIT

THE FRUIT OF FAITHFULNESS

"One who is faithful in a very little is also faithful in much,
and one who is dishonest in a very little is also dishonest in much."
Luke 16:10

faithfulness : commitment in relationship seen in loyalty & devotion.

In Jesus' parable above, the manager was proven to be unfaithful because he gave in to the temptation to mismanage what little he was given. Faithfulness is a virtue most reflected when we have to opportunity to be unfaithful.

We most often think of martial relationships when we talk about faithfulness, but friendships, familial and business relationships can also be affected by unfaithfulness.

Consistently choosing to remain faithful when given the opportunity to behave otherwise, builds our character and reputation.

* Have you ever been in a situation where you were tempted to be unfaithful?

* Did you seek the Holy Spirit in resisting the temptation?

* How did you respond? What was the result?

THE FRUIT OF GENTLENESS

"The Lord's servant must not quarrel, but be gentle towards all..."
2 Timothy 2:24

gentleness : softness of manners, mildness of temper, sweetness of disposition.

Interesting that the Greek word for gentle in 2 Timothy 2:24 only occurs one other place in the New Testament, and both references are to speech.

So we see that gentleness is not just visible in our demeanor, but reflected best in how we use our words in response to other.

• What does your tone of speech in response to others tell them about you?

"A soft answer turns away wrath, but a harsh word stirs up anger. The tongue of the wise commends knowledge, but the mouths of fools pour out folly." Proverbs 15:1-2

Even with the help of the Holy Spirit, we must still exercise our filter and choose which words to say and which to withhold. This includes non-verbal communication as well, like email and social media responses.

• What new habits might you need to put into practice (seeds to sow) to grow the fruit of gentleness?

Bearing Fruit : Living Rooted in Christ

THE FRUIT OF SELF-CONTROL

"Be sober-minded; be watchful. Your adversary the devil prowls around like a roaring lion, seeking someone to devour." 1 Peter 5:8

self-control : physical and emotional self mastery, particularly in situations of provocation and temptation.

In this example of self-control, Peter is urging the church to be sober-minded. He is not referring specifically to alcohol consumption but rather to the way being in a state of drunkenness causes us to loose control and can make us vulnerable to attacks by the enemy.

We are to be vigilant in keeping our passions and under restraint. This can even include anxiety.

"Therefore, preparing your minds for action, and being sober-minded, set your hope fully on the grace that will be brought to you at the revelation of Jesus Christ." 1 Peter 1:13

One of the best ways we can maintain our self-control, is to prepare ourselves. To keep our focus on God and to predetermine how we will and will not act or behave in a given situation, especially when provoked or tempted.

- Is there a particular area where you battle with self-control?

- Find a scripture that can encourage you, write it down and commit it to memory. Carry God's truth with you and be prepared when temptation comes.

the Fruit of the Spirit Galatians 5:22-23

Bearing Fruit : Living Rooted in Christ

PRAYER

BEARING FRUIT CHALLENGE

FRUIT	Seeds I will sow...
LOVE	
JOY	
PEACE	
PATIENCE	
KINDNESS	
GOODNESS	
FAITHFULNESS	
GENTLENESS	
SELF CONTROL	

Bearing Fruit : Living Rooted in Christ

Our challenge, is to be intentional about planting seeds and reaping the Fruit of the Spirit. Fill in the chart with the "seed" you intend to sow (be specific with how & who) for each fruit then return and notate the result.

Fruit I reaped....

Let Your Soul

Be Inspired!

VERSE MAPPING

No Good Tree BEARS BAD fruit nor does a bad tree BEAR good fruit FOR each tree is known by its own fruit

Luke 6: 43-44

FRUIT *NOT* OF THE SPIRIT

By: Stephanie K Adams, Real Women Ministries

> *"Now the works of the flesh are evident: sexual immorality, impurity, sensuality, idolatry, sorcery, enmity, strife, jealousy, fits of anger, rivalries, dissensions, divisions, envy, drunkenness, orgies, and things like these. I warn you, as I warned you before, that those who do such things will not inherit the kingdom of God."*
> Galatians 5:19-21

Since we have looked at what the fruit of the Spirit *is*, let's understand what it *is not* – for that we need to look at the verses prior to 22 and 23 in Galatians.

At first glance it looks like a pretty raunchy lifestyle, right?

But before we declare ourselves innocent of allowing our flesh to get in the way, let's breakdown a few of these, shall we?

IDOLATRY

If we are truly honest, we all have times when we put things ahead of God. We don't like to think of it as idolatry, but the Bible says:

> *"You shall have no other gods before me."*
> Exodus 20:3

Are we putting God second when we clearly feel the tug at our heart to open our Bible but we open social media instead?

Hello?! I know I can't be the only one, right?

- When you have "free time" during your day, what do you like to do?

- Which of the following things could be pruned back to create more (or any) free time in your day or week?

____ TV / movies   ____ social media   ____ email

____ hobbies   ____ shopping   ____ internet

____ _____   ____ _____   ____ _____

> **CHALLENGE:** *Prune your schedule to create 15 minutes of time to spend with God this week. Then next week, repeat this challenge daily.*

What about when we clearly hear Him whisper to speak to someone at the store, or reach out to someone from church, but instead we are afraid of what people will think of us, afraid we will be embarrassed. *Pride anyone?*

When we allow our agenda or feelings to take precedence over God's we are sowing seeds of the flesh.

- What ministries does your local church offer? Do they need assistance?

- Is there a local organization in need of volunteers?

> **CHALLENGE:** *Prune your schedule to create 30 minutes of time to spend assisting at your local church.*

If we want to become more intentional in our relationship with God and others, we are going to have to decide spending time with Him comes before all the other distractions. This is time He can speak to our heart about the plans He has, not solely for us personally, but also how we can serve Him by serving others.

- List 3 things you are doing or can begin doing to be intentional about spending time with God.

1.

2.

3.

Bearing Fruit : Living Rooted in Christ

ENMITY, STRIFE, DISSENSIONS, DIVISIONS

If you're like me you probably gloss right over enmity because you don't really know what it means.

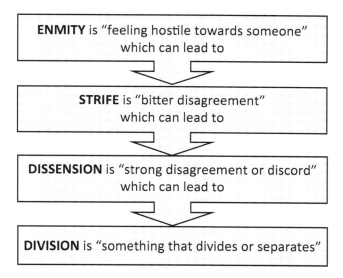

ENMITY is "feeling hostile towards someone" which can lead to

STRIFE is "bitter disagreement" which can lead to

DISSENSION is "strong disagreement or discord" which can lead to

DIVISION is "something that divides or separates"

Sadly, this happens all too often within the church walls. But it also happens in marriages, with kids, and with friends and family.

We find ourselves hostile about a situation and then engage in bitter disagreements, discord is fed and soon we find our relationships pulled apart.

How easily we can sow seeds of the flesh – often without realizing it.

• Review the chart again, do you currently find yourself in one of these boxes in a present relationship?

- Take some time with God right now and ask Him to reveal to you the seeds you have sown in this situation. Briefly note them below.

- What can you do to plant seeds of reconciliation?

"Love bears all things, believes all things, hopes all things, endures all things."
1 Corinthians 13:7

"Live in harmony with one another. Do not be haughty, but associate with the lowly. Never be wise in your own sight."
Romans 12:16

"First be reconciled to your brother, and then come and offer your gift."
Matthew 5:24b

Understanding how easily we can sow seeds of the flesh and reap fruit not of the spirit, makes it all the more important to become more intentional to sow seeds of the of Spirit, so we will begin reap the fruit of the Spirit in our lives.

> *"If we live by the Spirit,*
> *let us also keep in step with the Spirit."*
> Galatians 5:25

As we seek to become more intentional in our interactions, we hope it will encourage you to also find ways to be more purposeful in your own relationships.

It is our prayer that you will allow God to grow those seeds of faith in your life – *so you can begin sowing a legacy of Jesus in the lives around you.*

Jesus, help us to seek You first in everything we do. May we see You in the faces we pass each day; may we hear Your voice as you speak opportunities to serve others; and may we find our faith growing ever stronger as we become more intentional in our relationships. Help us to slow our pace so we can see You in all we do.....

In Jesus' name, Amen.

Let Your Soul

Be Inspired!

THAT'S A WRAP

Soul Friends, I have so enjoyed the journey through our study with you. I have learned so much about Bearing Fruit and am recommitted to staying rooted in Christ, our spiritual life source.

In closing, I would like to leave you with this encouragement from Pastor Paul Fritz, an excerpt from his sermon, *12 Types of Spiritual Fruit.*

> ALLOW THE COMFORTING MINISTRY OF THE HOLY SPIRIT TO HELP YOU BEAR FRUIT IN EVERY GOOD WORK AS YOU INCREASE IN THE KNOWLEDGE OF GOD AND EXPERIENCE MORE OF HIS HELP, COMFORT, INTERCESSION, WISDOM, TRUTH AND LOVE EVERYDAY IN EVERY WAY.

Let's hold on to the truths from God's Word about His faithfulness and continue to pray with the expectation of God delivering an answer to those prayers.

Blessings Soul Friends,

Other Soul Deep Devotionals & Journals from
Sweet To The Soul Ministries

31-Day Devotionals
Let Your Light Shine : Being a Light in a Dark World

31-Day Scripture Journals
New Life

Love Is

Grace

God's Masterpiece

I Believe

Let Your Light Shine

Everyday Thanksgiving

Anchored Hope

7-Day Scripture Journals
Together We're Better

Rest for the Weary Soul

Every Good Gift

For more information visit:
SweetToTheSoul.com/Soul-Deep-Books

Other Soul Inspired Products from
Sweet To The Soul Ministries

Coloring Books
Garden of Life

Bible Study / Journaling Kits
Anchored Hope
Joy Filled Life

Bible Journaling Templates /
Color Your Own Bookmarks

Color Pages & Prints

Bible Journaling / Crafting
Digital Kits
Gods' Masterpiece

For more information visit:
SweetToTheSoul.com/Soul-Inspired

Or

Visit our Etsy shop at
www.etsy.com/shop/SweetToTheSoulShoppe

MEET THE AUTHORS

Jana Kennedy-Spicer is a wife, mom and Nana who is passionate about inspiring and encouraging women on their daily walk with Christ. A woman rescued and repaired by the grace of God, she loves to share about the realness of God's love, redemption and faithfulness. Embarking on a new life journey, she is dedicated to using her blogging, Bible teaching, writing, photography, drawing, painting and graphic designs to bring glory to the Lord.

Jana teaches Bible Study and Bible Journaling in the Dallas, Texas area. To connect with Jana at www.SweetToTheSoul.com.

Stephanie K. Adams is a writer, speaker and founder of REAL Women Ministries, where a community of women gather to grow their Relationship with each other and God through Encouragement and Accountability to studying the Bible, and cultivating a Love for His Word. Stephanie'S writings have been featured at The Blythe Daniel Agency's Blog Spot, Chosen and Crowned Ministries, 818 Ministries, and Triple Negative Breast Cancer Foundation. Stephanie enjoys reading, a good cup of coffee, and Saturday breakfast with her husband, Rick. To connect with Stephanie and join a community of real women studying God's Word, visit www.RealWomenMinistries.org

Copy, color and gift these tags to inspire someone's day.

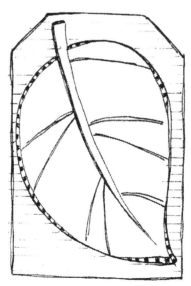

Printed in Great Britain
by Amazon